ANIMAL
BABIES

This 1996 edition is published by Derrydale Books,
a division of Random House Value Publishing, Inc.,
40 Engelhard Avenue, Avenel, New Jersey 07001.

Random House
New York • Toronto • London • Sydney • Auckland
http://www.randomhouse.com/

ISBN 0-517-15996-1

Conceived, edited, and designed by McRae Books, Florence, Italy
Illustrations: Fiammetta Dogi
Text: Beatrice MacLeod
Design: Marco Nardi

Printed and bound in Italy

8 7 6 5 4 3 2 1

ANIMAL BABIES

Illustrated by
Fiammetta Dogi

DERRYDALE BOOKS
New York • Avenel

Baby caterpillar hatches from an egg his mother laid on some tasty cabbage leaves.

Just Born

Finally, after weeks, months, or even years of waiting, the baby animal is born. Some babies can take care of themselves soon after birth. Others stay with their families until they learn how to survive on their own.

Father seahorse keeps his babies safe in a special pouch on his stomach.

Mother elephant waits for nearly two years before her calf is born. She spends several years teaching it how to take care of itself.

Some fish hold their eggs in their mouths until the little ones hatch.

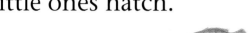

This little turtle has just broken the soft, leathery shell covering its egg.

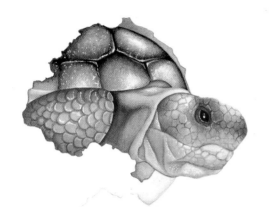

Zebra foals struggle to their feet just a few minutes after birth. They learn to run quickly, so that they can escape from predators.

Baby birds, like this ostrich hatchling, use their beaks to break out of their hard egg shells.

A busy worker ant hauls food to its nest for baby ants to eat.

Eating

Young animals need lots of good food to help them grow. Many animal parents hunt for their offspring until they learn to feed themselves.

Baby seagull knows that if he taps the red spot on his mother's beak she will give him food.

Mammal mothers feed their babies on milk. This doe will suckle her fawn for several months.

Baboons love to eat ostrich eggs. This little baboon has stolen an egg from a nest.

Chimpanzees like to eat termites. This young chimp has already learned how to dig them out of an old tree trunk using a stick.

This jaguar cub licks her lips after a big meal of fresh meat. Her mother hunts for her.

Squirrels eat seeds, nuts, fruit, and leaves. This little red squirrel is clasping a nut.

Thrush chicks wait impatiently for their parents to bring food.

Puppies that live indoors need to take a bath to keep clean.

Keeping Clean

Animals care for their fur, feathers, or skin by grooming regularly. Mothers often groom their babies when they are small. This not only keeps them clean, it also creates a strong bond between parent and offspring.

Mother baboon removes pests from her baby. Monkeys and apes groom each other even when they are full grown.

Birds, like this duckling, use their beaks to clean themselves. This is called preening.

Cats are very clean animals. Mother cats groom their kittens every day as they grow. With such a good example, kittens soon learn to keep themselves clean.

Some animals help keep others clean. Baby giraffe has three oxpeckers on his back. They remove blood-sucking ticks and flies from his hide.

Baby elephant has already learned how to spray herself with refreshing water. This keeps her clean and cool, and soothes her sensitive skin.

Baby chimpanzee sits quietly resting.

Resting

Many baby animals spend almost all their time sleeping. As they grow they spend more time playing, learning, and searching for food.

This little seal is snoozing peacefully. His mother is always near to keep watch.

When cygnets are tired of swimming they climb onto their mother's back and enjoy the ride.

Animals sleep when they feel safe. Mother gorilla rests while her baby looks on.

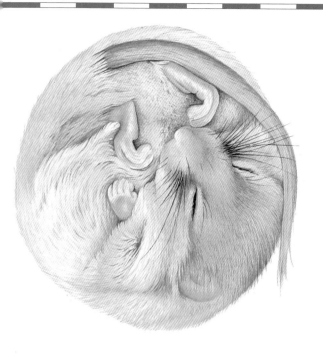

In fall young dormice settle down for a long sleep. They don't wake up again until spring. This is called hibernation.

Newborn mammals only wake up long enough to feed. These rabbits snuggle up in their soft, downy nest. They keep each other warm.

Kittens sleep almost the whole time. Even full-grown cats spend about half their lives sleeping.

Some caterpillars eat poisonous flowers. They become poisonous too, and birds are afraid to eat them.

Keeping Safe

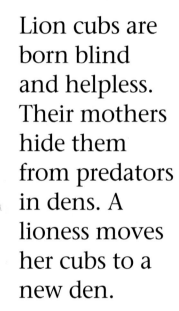

Animals always keep a watch out for predators. Young animals are often too weak or slow to protect themselves. Their parents keep them safe.

Lion cubs are born blind and helpless. Their mothers hide them from predators in dens. A lioness moves her cubs to a new den.

Newly hatched bantam chicks snuggle up to their mother for warmth. There are many more chicks under mother hen.

Koalas live in the trees. Young koalas cling to their mother's back until they can climb alone.

Newborn grazing animals, like this gazelle calf, can keep up with the herd just twenty minutes after birth.

Little ring-tailed lemurs travel piggyback on their mothers for the first months of their lives. During this time they learn how to survive by themselves.

Keeping close to a parent is always the best way to stay out of harm's way. Baby frog rides on its parent's head.

Mother shield bug keeps her babies in a tight group.

Wild boars have three or four piglets at a time.

Families

Many animals grow up in a family. Some families are small, with just mother and one baby. Others are large, and include numerous offspring, mother, father, aunts, and other caretakers.

Albatrosses lay only one egg, so they never have more than one chick at a time.

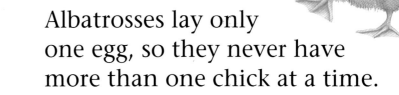

In spring mother grizzly emerges from her winter den with two or three cubs.

Baby owls huddle up to their mother to keep warm. Young owls live with their parents for several months before flying away to make their own homes.

Australian wild dogs, called dingoes, have large families. Sometimes there are as many as ten or twelve puppies in a litter.

Emperor penguins don't make nests. Instead, father penguin keeps the egg on his feet for two months. When it hatches mother penguin returns from the sea with fish to feed her family.

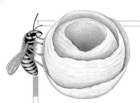

Queen wasps build nests to lay their eggs in.

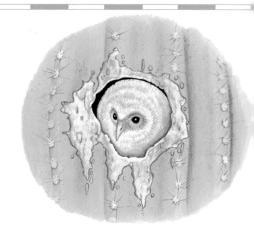

Homes

Finding a place to live is important for many animals, particularly if they are about to become parents. They need a warm, safe place where they can bring up their young.

Baby owl peeps out of a hole in a cactus. Her mother built their home in an old woodpecker nest.

Fox cubs are born in dens their mother makes for them under tree roots or in old logs. Mother fox and other female helpers carry food to the cubs until they are big enough to come out.

Most birds build nests where they can lay their eggs and bring up their chicks. This is a hanging nest made by weaver birds.

Most monkeys spend all their lives in the treetops. This little monkey is already a skillful climber.

Hyena pups live in a big underground den with all the other babies in their group. Their mother feeds them milk for up to fifteen months.

Many squirrels make their dens in old hollow trees. These are good, snug places to bring up babies.

Baby parrot is learning to fly.

Learning

Animals know some things when they are born, by instinct. But they also learn by playing, exploring, and imitating their parents.

Mountain goats learn to jump when they are just a few weeks old.

Kittens are curious. They sniff and prod at almost everything. This is how they learn about the world.

Mother hedgehog takes her babies with her when she goes hunting. They learn how to catch insects and worms.

Baby dolphins are born underwater. They know how to swim by instinct, so they don't need to learn.

Puppies are playful.
They love to wrestle.
This helps them grow strong.

Like us, animals can also learn by observing the world around them.

Birds sing songs to warn each other of danger or to keep in touch.

Talking

Animals talk to each other and communicate by making sounds, leaving smells, or by making signals with their bodies.

Ducklings make "cheep cheep" noises when they are tiny. As they grow up, they learn to make loud "quacking" sounds.

Whales sing songs under the sea. They boom out loud calls that travel across the ocean depths to other whales.

Prairie dogs are not really dogs. They are rodents. They get their name from the loud, dog-like barks they make even when they are young.

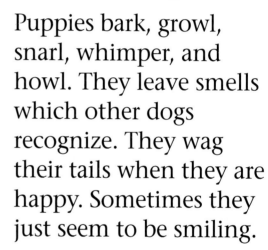

Mother sheep, called ewes, know their own lamb's calls among all the others. They also recognize their baby by its smell.

Puppies bark, growl, snarl, whimper, and howl. They leave smells which other dogs recognize. They wag their tails when they are happy. Sometimes they just seem to be smiling.

Young jellyfish swim by
pulsating their bell-shaped tops.

Amazing Babies

The animal kingdom is full of
surprises. Some babies look
strange and awkward, but they
grow up to be healthy adults
just the same.

Armadillos have scales
and armor to protect
them from predators.
They develop their
protective suits quite
soon after birth.

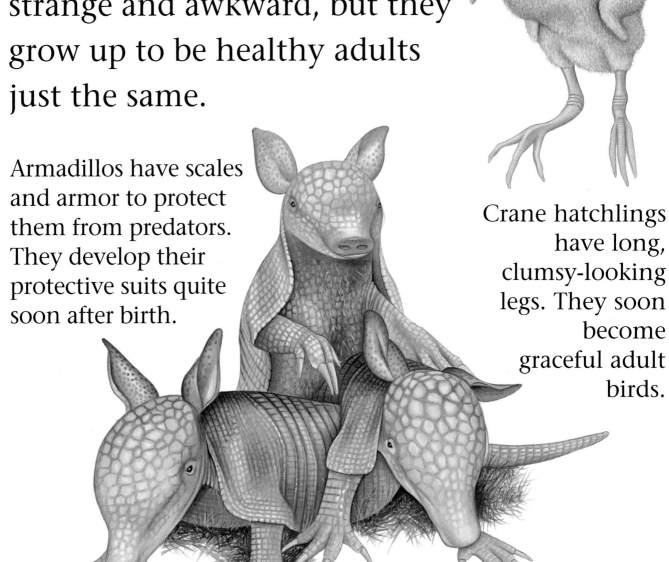

Crane hatchlings
have long,
clumsy-looking
legs. They soon
become
graceful adult
birds.

Cats and dogs that grow up together sometimes become best friends.

Baby tapirs have white stripes and blotches on their fur. These fade away as they grow up.

Kangaroos normally have brown fur. This joey is milk-white. He is an albino. Albino babies have pink skin, white hair or fur, and red eyes. They stay white all their lives.

Newborn aardvarks have no hair on their bodies. They have long snouts and large, floppy ears.

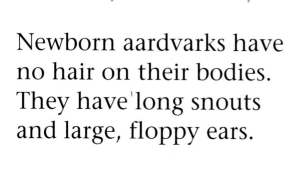

In the fall caterpillars turn into chrysalises.

When tadpoles grow up, they turn into frogs.

Growing Up

As animal babies grow they begin to take care of themselves. They learn how to hunt for food and how to avoid predators.

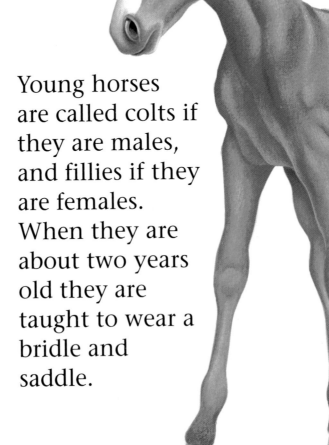

Young horses are called colts if they are males, and fillies if they are females. When they are about two years old they are taught to wear a bridle and saddle.

Penguin chicks are almost as large as their parents before their soft down feathers are replaced by adult plumage.

Learning to fly is a big step for young birds. They leave the nest and their families soon afterward. This eaglet is almost ready to test his wings.

This bison calf has just been weaned. From now on she will feed on grass.

Young raccoons, called kits, learn to catch fish by watching their mothers closely. At first they are too clumsy to catch anything, but with time they become good hunters.

Hamsters are rodents. They make good pets.

Full Grown

Sooner or later animal babies become adults. Then they are ready to give birth to and bring up babies of their own.

This butterfly fish has a dark spot like an eye near its tail. This frightens predators away.

Male lions have magnificent shaggy manes. They are sometimes called the king of beasts.

A full-grown male rhinoceros can weigh as much as a family car.

Toucans live in tropical rain forests. They have brightly colored bills which they use to eat fruit and insects.

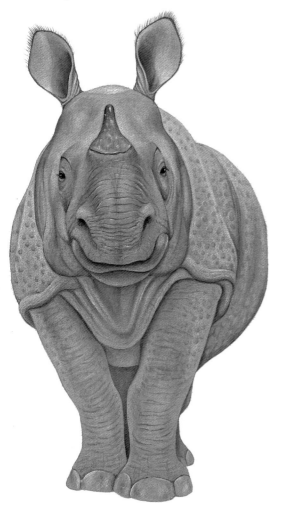

When they are about three months old, tadpoles grow legs, leave the water, and become frogs. They feed on insects.

In spring adult butterflies hatch from chrysalises. They feed on the nectar they find in flowers.

Index